Welcome to the Home Study Collection™ created because we believe that the home is a child's first and most important teacher.

Dear Friend,

To succeed in math, learners need to understand concepts as well as perform calculations.

*Math and More* is designed to help your learner develop and apply both thinking and math skills.

Each book includes—

    * interesting, grade-appropriate math lessons

    * activities that give practice in important math skills

    * activities that encourage both practical and creative use of math concepts

    * an achievement certificate for the young learner who completes the book

In addition, the book includes a convenient pull-out section with the following items—

    * an answer key for each activity

    * an easy-to-use skills chart

    * suggestions for working with young learners

We hope that you and your learner will enjoy the learning experiences found in

*Math and More.*

Sincerely,

ECS Home Study Team

ISBN 1-57022-037-9
Edited by Lori Mammen
Page Layout and Graphics by Julie Gumm
Cover and Book design by Educational Media Services
Art on pages 1, 3, 6, 7, 14, 17, 22, 43, 47, 48, 50, 52, 54 by Corel GALLERY

# Number Patterns

A number pattern is a series of numbers that follows a rule. The rule for the following pattern is "subtract 6." To find the next number in the pattern you must follow the rule.

39    33    27    21    15

The following pattern has two rules: "add 1, then multiply by 2." What is the next number in the pattern?

3    4    8    9    18    19    38    _____

✎ Write the missing numbers in each pattern.

1.  17    21    25    _____    _____    37    _____

2.  6    5    8    7    10    9    _____    _____    _____

3.  3    _____    27    81    _____

4.  2    5    5    8    8    11    _____    _____    _____

5.  210    200    _____    _____    170    160    _____    _____

6.  1    4    9    _____    25    36    _____    _____

✎ Write the missing numbers in the pattern. Then write the pattern's rule.

1    3    6    8    _____    _____    36    38

_____

_____

_____

- Solve the word problem. Work in the space.

  Sarah was helping her mother arrange fruit in baskets. Sarah placed 1 apple and 2 oranges in the first basket, 2 apples and 4 oranges in the second basket, and 4 apples and 8 oranges in the third basket. To continue the pattern, what combination of fruit would Sarah place in the fourth and fifth baskets?

- Choose 2 rules from the following list. Then build a pattern using those rules.

  | multiply by 3 | divide by 3 | multiply by 4 |
  | divide by 2 | subtract 7 | subtract 5 |
  | add 9 | add 10 | add 8 |

  _____

  _____

 Design a secret code that is based on a number pattern. Use the code to write a message to your parents. Can they "crack" the code?

# Translating Numbers

Numbers can be written as numerals or as words.

✎ Write the numerals.

1.  one million, three hundred forty-three thousand, one hundred one

    _____

2.  three million, four hundred five thousand, two hundred ten

    _____

3.  nine hundred thousand, four hundred twenty-one

    _____

4.  one million, fifty-two thousand, five hundred eighty-one

    _____

✎ Write the number words.

5.  The new convention center cost the city $4,986,110.

    _____

6.  The bank loaned $368,900 to the company. _____

    _____

7.  Our town has a population of 8,321. _____

    _____

8.  The astronauts traveled 31,585 miles. _____

    _____

• You are planning a vacation to several different cities. Use a map to find the distance from your home to each of the following cities. Write each distance as a numeral and as words.

| City | Distance (Numeral) | Distance (Words) |
|------|--------------------|--------------------|
| Chicago | | |
| New York | | |
| San Francisco | | |
| New Orleans | | |

• If you traveled to each city and back, how many miles would you travel in all? Write the distance as a numeral and as words.

_____

_____

_____

 When do people usually write numbers as words? as numerals? Why? Talk to your mom or dad and find out when they write numbers as words.

# Place Value

We use 10 digits (1,2,3,4,5,6,7,8,9,0) to make every number. A digit's place, or position, shows its value in a number.

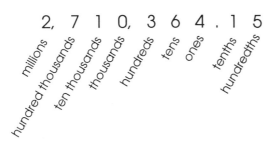

✎ Write the answers.

1.  What is the value of 2 in 2,980,764?_____

2.  What is the value of 1 in 468,392.15?_____

3.  What is the value of 6 in 1,006,478?_____

4.  What is the value of 9 in 56,901.46?_____

5.  What is the value of of 6 in 41.63?_____

6.  What is the value of 8 in 9,144.38?_____

✎ Mark the correct answer with a check mark.

7.  Which number has a 5 in the ones place and a 2 in the thousands place?

    ❏ 6,327,915         ❏ 6,273,159
    ❏ 6,732,195         ❏ 6,732,519

8.  Which number has a 6 in the hundredths place and a 4 in the hundreds place?

    ❏ 5,147.62          ❏ 5,417.26
    ❏ 5,147.26          ❏ 5,417.62

- What is the value of 7 in each of the following numbers?

  1. 7,140.06 _____

  2. 700,000 _____

  3. 147.36 _____

  4. 474,365 _____

  5. 1,000,000.07 _____

  6. 1,000,000.7 _____

  7. 417.0 _____

  8. 97,634.5 _____

- Write a 5-digit number that has a 6 in the hundreds place.

  _____

  Write a 6-digit number that has a 1 in the thousands place.

  _____

  There is a 4 in the tenths place; a 6 in the thousands place; an 8 in the hundreds place; a 1 in the tens place; and a 3 in the ones place.

  What is the number? _____

🏠 Play this game with one of your parents. You will need 2 dice, paper, and pencil. Each person draws the following game board on paper: $ _____ _____ _____ . _____ _____ . The first player throws a die and writes the number shown in one of the game board's blanks. The second player does the same. Play continues until both players have filled in their game boards. Player with the greater amount wins the round. Play 10 rounds.

# Rounding

Rounding is one way to estimate or to know about how many. Look at the examples.

      Round 315 to the nearest hundred.

To round to the nearest hundred, look at the tens digit. It is less than 5. The hundreds digit stays at 3 and the other digits are changed to 0. 315 rounded to the nearest hundred is 300.

      Round 365 to the nearest hundred.

Look at the tens digit. It is greater than 5. Add 1 to the hundreds place. 365 rounded to the nearest hundred is 400.

✏ Round to the nearest thousand.

1.  6,713 _____
2.  1,010 _____
3.  5,632 _____
4.  36,417 _____
5.  110,900 _____
6.  111,056 _____

✏ Round to the nearest ten thousand.

7.  89,164 _____
8.  76,410 _____
9.  81,968 _____
10. 67,000 _____
11. 78,094 _____
12. 126,078 _____

✏ Round to the nearest hundred thousand.

13. 403,987 _____
14. 391,400 _____
15. 1,201,967 _____
16. 2,960,814 _____

- Look at the population chart. Complete the chart by rounding each population to the nearest million.

| State | Population | Rounded Population |
|---|---|---|
| Alabama | 3,893,888 | |
| California | 23,667,565 | |
| Connecticut | 3,107,576 | |
| Hawaii | 964,691 | |
| Illinois | 11,426,518 | |
| Minnesota | 4,075,970 | |
| New Mexico | 1,302,981 | |
| Texas | 14,229,288 | |

Which states have about 4 times as many people as New Mexico?

_____

Which state has about the same number of people as Hawaii?

_____

 Ask your mom or dad to explain when they use rounding. Can you think of other times when rounding is a good way to estimate?

# Review

Solve each problem and circle the letter that matches a correct response. Unscramble the circled letters to find the name of a large city in the United States.

1.  6      16      26      _____      46

2.  3      9      10      30      31      _____      94

3.  1      4      _____      16      25      36

4.  4      6      5      7      6      _____      7

5.  _____      111      121      131      141

6.  1      3      3      5      5      _____

7.  6      9      12      _____      18      21

8.  4      8      12      16      _____      24

9.  1      8      _____      64      125

10. 1      4      3      12      11      _____      43

| 101 | 7 | 9 | 32 | 36 | 20 | 6 | 44 | 91 | 93 | 48 | 8 | 90 | 15 | 27 | 80 |
|-----|---|---|----|----|----|---|----|----|----|----|---|----|----|----|----|
| A | O | L | T | E | L | H | S | U | G | M | N | C | E | S | G |

_____

Answer each problem. Then add all the answers together. If you have answered correctly, the sum of the answers will be 1,000,000.

1. Write three hundred ten thousand, two hundred fifteen as a

   numeral. _____

2. Write twenty-seven thousand, two hundred as a numeral.

   _____

3. Which number has a 6 in the hundreds place: 126,120 or
   121,620?

   _____

4. Which number has a 1 in the ten thousands place: 381,452 or
   314,548?

   _____

5. Round 117,461 to the nearest thousand. _____

6. Round 56,096 to the nearest hundred. _____

7. Round 946 to the nearest thousand. _____

8. Round 21,416 to the nearest ten. _____

9. Round 27,010 to the nearest ten thousand. _____

10. Write the number that has a 7 in the ones place, an 8 in the

    hundreds place, and a 9 in the tens place. _____

# Number Lines: Decimals

A number line shows numbers in order from least to greatest. A number line lets you compare numbers. The following number line shows numbers from 0 to 1.0.

0   0.1  0.2  0.3  0.4  0.5  0.6  0.7  0.8  0.9  1.0

The number line shows that 0.2 is less 0.8. In math, you write it this way: 0.2 < 0.8.

✎ Fill in the missing numbers on the number lines.

1.

0  0.5  1.0  1.5          3.0  3.5

2.

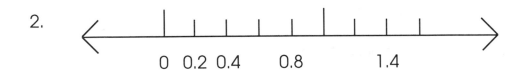

0  0.2  0.4      0.8          1.4

✎ Write the symbol < (less than) or > (greater than) to make each of the following number sentences true.

3.  0.5  ◯  1.0              7.  0.6  ◯  0.2

4.  0.4  ◯  0               8.  1.0  ◯  0.5

5.  3.5  ◯  3.0             9.  0.8  ◯  1.0

6.  1.2  ◯  1.4            10.  1.6  ◯  1.2

- The chart shows the average rainfall in several cities during January and February.

| ✓ Dallas, Texas | 1.8 inches |
| ✗ Chicago, Illinois | 1.5 inches |
| ✦ Boise, Idaho | 1.4 inches |
| ★ Helena, Montana | 0.6 inches |
| ■ Minneapolis, Minnesota | 0.9 inches |
| ❤ Oklahoma City, Oklahoma | 1.2 inches |
| ➜ Phoenix, Arizona | 0.7 inches |
| ✚ Reno, Nevada | 1.1 inches |

Place the rainfall amounts on the number line. Write the city's symbol above the correct amount of rainfall.

Find at least 10 canned foods that have different weights (use metric weight). Arrange the items from least to greatest weight. Can you make a number line that shows the weight of each can?

# Comparing Decimals

To compare decimals, compare the digits in the tenths place first. If the digits in the tenths place are the same, compare the digits in the hundredths place.

$$0.5 \ > 0.1 \qquad \text{Compare the tenths.}$$
$$0.54 > 0.51 \qquad \text{Compare the hundredths.}$$

Circle the decimal that is greater.

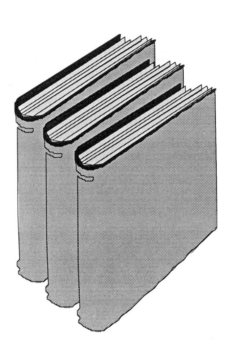

1.  0.15      0.05

2.  0.6       0.7

3.  0.11      0.12

4.  0.48      0.58

5.  0.9       0.89

6.  0.2       0.19

7.  0.31      0.33

8.  0.7       0.68

Write the symbol < (less than) or > (greater than) to make each of the following number sentences true.

9.  0.12 ◯ 0.15      13.  0.93 ◯ 0.91

10.  0.7 ◯ 0.65      14.  0.47 ◯ 0.51

11.  0.25 ◯ 0.2      15.  0.03 ◯ 0.12

12.  0.36 ◯ 0.41      16.  0.09 ◯ 0.08

• Mrs. Davidson, the librarian, has several new books to shelf. Each book has a special number that includes a decimal. Mrs. Davidson must place the books on the shelf from least to greatest, according to their numbers. Can you help her? Number the books in the correct order.

301.12    212.13    151.12    151.09

116.4    911.24    800.56    792.44

331.56    212.2    116.42    664.81

🏠 Visit a library with one of your parents. Ask the librarian about the Dewey Decimal System and how it is used.

# Fractions

Fractions are numbers that describe parts of a whole. Look at the example.

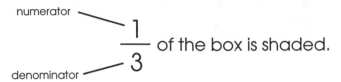

$\dfrac{1}{3}$ of the box is shaded.

A fraction has a denominator and a numerator. The denominator tells the total number of equal pieces in the whole. The numerator tells how many of the equal pieces are in the number. Look at the example again. It was divided into 3 equal sections. The denominator is 3. Only 1 section has been shaded. The numerator is 1.

 Divide and shade each box to show the fraction.

$\dfrac{2}{4}$

$\dfrac{3}{8}$

$\dfrac{2}{3}$

$\dfrac{1}{10}$

$\dfrac{3}{5}$

$\dfrac{3}{4}$

$\dfrac{1}{6}$

$\dfrac{5}{6}$

- Look at the chart and answer the questions.

Neighborhood Pets

|  | Dogs | Cats | Hamsters | Fish |
|---|---|---|---|---|
| McGuire Family | 2 | 0 | 1 | 0 |
| Jackson Family | 1 | 1 | 0 | 0 |
| Evans Family | 2 | 2 | 1 | 0 |
| Martinez Family | 0 | 0 | 2 | 5 |
| Wong Family | 1 | 1 | 1 | 1 |

1. What fraction of the McGuires' pets are dogs? _____
2. What fraction of the Wongs' pets are fish? _____
3. What fraction of the Martinez family's pets are hamsters? _____
4. What fraction of the Evans family's pets are cats? _____
5. What fraction of the Jacksons' pets are dogs? _____
6. Which family owns 2/5 of all the hamsters? _____
7. Which family owns 1/6 of all the fish? _____
8. What fraction of all the families own dogs? _____
9. What fraction of all the families own cats? _____
10. What fraction of all the families own hamsters? _____
11. What fraction of all the families own fish? _____
12. The Martinez family owns the greatest number of pets. What fraction of all the neighborhood pets do they own? _____

 Make a neighborhood pet chart like the one above, but record the pets that some of your neighbors own. Write the fractions that describe how many of your neighbors' pets are dogs, cats, hamsters, or fish. Ask your parents to help you.

# Comparing Fractions

To compare fractions with the same denominator, look at the numerator.

$$\frac{1}{3} < \frac{2}{3}$$

To compare fractions with different denominators, you must rewrite the fractions so that they have common denominators.

$$\frac{3}{4} \; \textcircled{?} \; \frac{1}{2}$$

Ask: How many fourths equal $\frac{1}{2}$ ?

Express $\frac{1}{2}$ in fourths: $\frac{1}{2} \times \frac{2}{2} = \frac{2}{4}$

Compare the fractions: $\frac{3}{4} > \frac{2}{4}$

✎ Write the symbol < (less than), > (greater than), or = (equals) to make each of the following number sentences true.

1. $\frac{2}{5} \bigcirc \frac{3}{5}$

2. $\frac{1}{10} \bigcirc \frac{2}{10}$

3. $\frac{3}{6} \bigcirc \frac{1}{2}$

4. $\frac{2}{5} \bigcirc \frac{3}{10}$

5. $\frac{2}{6} \bigcirc \frac{6}{12}$

6. $\frac{3}{8} \bigcirc \frac{1}{4}$

7. $\frac{2}{6} \bigcirc \frac{1}{3}$

8. $\frac{4}{15} \bigcirc \frac{3}{5}$

9. $\frac{1}{2} \bigcirc \frac{2}{6}$

10. $\frac{4}{8} \bigcirc \frac{1}{2}$

11. $\frac{2}{3} \bigcirc \frac{7}{9}$

12. $\frac{1}{3} \bigcirc \frac{3}{9}$

• Greg, Teddy, Mike, and Jimmy each bought a candy bar at the movie theater. Each candy bar was the same size, but each one had a different number of sections. Look at the chart to find out more about the boys' candy bars and how much they ate. Then answer the questions.

|  | Total Number of Sections | Sections Eaten |
|---|---|---|
| Greg | 6 | 2 |
| Teddy | 3 | 2 |
| Mike | 2 | 1 |
| Jimmy | 4 | 1 |

1. What fraction of his candy bar did each boy eat?

   Greg _____    Teddy _____    Mike _____    Jimmy _____

2. Which boy ate the most candy? _____

3. Which boy ate the least candy? _____

4. True or False: Greg ate more candy than Jimmy. _____

5. True or False: Mike ate more candy than Greg. _____

6. True or False: Teddy ate more candy than Mike. _____

7. True or False: Greg ate more candy than Mike. _____

8. True or False: Jimmy ate more candy than Teddy. _____

Ask your mom or dad to give you some plastic cups and containers of different sizes. Use the cups and containers to work with fractions. For example, can you figure out which cup or container is about 1/3 the size of another? Can you figure out which cup or container is about 1/2 the size of another? Explain your work to your mom or dad.

# Writing Fractions in Lowest Terms

The fraction 1/3 is in lowest terms. Its numerator and denominator can only be divided by 1.

The fraction 2/4 is not in lowest terms. Its numerator and denominator can be divided by 1 and by 2. Look at the example.

$$\frac{2}{4} \div \frac{2}{2} = \frac{1}{2}$$

A fraction is in lowest terms when the numerator and denominator can only be divided by 1.

 Circle the fractions that are written in lowest terms.

1. $\dfrac{2}{5}$     2. $\dfrac{2}{6}$     3. $\dfrac{2}{10}$     4. $\dfrac{3}{9}$

5. $\dfrac{2}{3}$     6. $\dfrac{7}{9}$     7. $\dfrac{3}{6}$     8. $\dfrac{6}{12}$

9. $\dfrac{4}{5}$     10. $\dfrac{3}{5}$     11. $\dfrac{4}{8}$     12. $\dfrac{3}{4}$

 Rewrite each fraction in lowest terms.

13. $\dfrac{4}{12}$     14. $\dfrac{6}{12}$     15. $\dfrac{4}{6}$     16. $\dfrac{6}{9}$

17. $\dfrac{5}{10}$     18. $\dfrac{2}{10}$     19. $\dfrac{3}{12}$     20. $\dfrac{6}{15}$

21. $\dfrac{2}{8}$     22. $\dfrac{3}{9}$     23. $\dfrac{10}{15}$     24. $\dfrac{6}{8}$

- Barbara's friend gave her the recipe for a great cake, but Barbara didn't have the same kind of measuring cups and spoons as her friend. Help Barbara by figuring out which of her measuring cups and spoons she should use.

Ingredients:

3/12 cup of butter              6/9 cup of white sugar
5/20 cup of milk                6/8 teaspoon of baking powder
2/4 cup of nuts                 6/24 teaspoon of salt
3/9 cup of brown sugar          2 and 6/24  cups of flour

Barbara's measuring cups and spoons:

1/4 cup, 1/3 cup, 1/2 cup, 2/3 cup, 3/4 cup, 1 cup,
1/4 teaspoon, 1/2 teaspoon, 3/4 teaspoon, 1 teaspoon

Write the measuring cup or spoon that Barbara should use to measure:

the butter _____

the milk _____

the nuts _____

the brown sugar _____

the white sugar _____

the baking powder _____

the salt _____

the flour _____

 Use a set of kitchen measuring cups and measuring spoons to learn more about fractions. For example, how many different ways can you measure 1/2 cup? How many different ways can you measure 1/4 cup? How many different ways can you measure 1/2 teaspoon? Ask your mom or dad to help you.

# Review

Compare each pair of decimals. Circle the letter written under the greater decimal in each pair. Write the circled letters on the line. Unscramble the letters to spell the name of a continent.

1.  0.45          0.4
    R             S

2.  2.2           2.15
    U             T

3.  0.09          0.11
    M             L

4.  0.56          0.55
    S             N

5.  1.06          1.16
    E             A

6.  2.22          2.06
    A             P

7.  0.06          0.07
    H             T

8.  0.1           0.09
    I             E

9.  3.0           3.01
    U             A

_____

_____

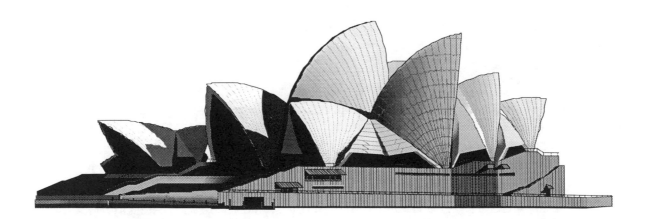

None of the following fractions are in lowest terms. Write each fraction on the chart under the fraction that expresses each one in lowest terms.

$\dfrac{2}{6}$      $\dfrac{3}{9}$      $\dfrac{6}{12}$      $\dfrac{4}{6}$      $\dfrac{2}{4}$      $\dfrac{3}{12}$

$\dfrac{5}{10}$      $\dfrac{4}{12}$      $\dfrac{6}{9}$      $\dfrac{12}{16}$      $\dfrac{2}{8}$      $\dfrac{6}{15}$

$\dfrac{15}{20}$      $\dfrac{9}{12}$      $\dfrac{3}{6}$      $\dfrac{2}{10}$

| $\dfrac{1}{2}$ | $\dfrac{1}{3}$ | $\dfrac{2}{3}$ | $\dfrac{1}{4}$ | $\dfrac{3}{4}$ | $\dfrac{1}{5}$ | $\dfrac{2}{5}$ |
|---|---|---|---|---|---|---|
|  |  |  |  |  |  |  |
|  |  |  |  |  |  |  |
|  |  |  |  |  |  |  |
|  |  |  |  |  |  |  |

Compare each set of fractions. Circle the letter under the greater fraction. Unscramble the circled letters to find the name of a city in the United States.

1. $\dfrac{2}{5}$      $\dfrac{3}{5}$          2. $\dfrac{2}{5}$      $\dfrac{3}{10}$          3. $\dfrac{1}{2}$      $\dfrac{2}{6}$
   N      I            M     U          A     E

4. $\dfrac{1}{4}$      $\dfrac{3}{8}$          5. $\dfrac{2}{3}$      $\dfrac{7}{9}$
   P      I            T     M

# Operations Practice

You should know how to add, subtract, multiply, and divide whole numbers.

 Add or subtract.

| | | | |
|---|---|---|---|
| 1.    864<br>    + 738 | 2.    1099<br>    + 872 | 3.    4710<br>    − 1852 | 4.    5148<br>    + 4894 |

| | | | |
|---|---|---|---|
| 5.    907<br>    − 159 | 6.    7510<br>    − 4607 | 7.    999<br>    + 101 | 8.    3066<br>    − 1847 |

 Multiply or divide.

| | | | |
|---|---|---|---|
| 9.    73<br>   x 29 | 10.    807<br>    x 34 | 11.    600<br>    x 10 | 12.    971<br>    x 69 |

13.   7$\overline{)806}$      14.   3$\overline{)7184}$      15.   14$\overline{)7002}$

16.   23$\overline{)6946}$      17.   16$\overline{)1000}$      18.   4$\overline{)4172}$

- Solve the following word problems.

1. Carrie's family took a trip. On the first day they drove 120 km. On the second day they drove 153 km, and on the third day they drove 178 km. How many kilometers did they drive in 3 days?

   _____ km

2. Chris practiced his trumpet for 30 minutes each day. How many minutes did he practice in 2 weeks?

   _____ minutes

3. A movie theater holds 986 seats. If 338 seats were empty during the first show, how many tickets had been sold?

   _____ tickets

4. A museum had 848 visitors to a special exhibit. If visitors toured the exhibit in groups of 16, how many groups took the tour?

   _____ groups

- Place the correct operation signs (+, –, x, ÷) for each problem.

5. 92 ◯ 86 = 7912

6. 462 ◯ 21 = 22

7. 569 ◯ 263 – 129 = 703

8. 500 ◯ 234 ◯ 697 = 963

9. 42 ◯ 16 ◯ 6 = 112

10. 2236 ◯ 52 ◯ 21 = 903

🏠 Ask your parents how they use addition, subtraction, multiplication, and division each day.

# Adding & Subtracting Decimals

To add or subtract decimals, first line up the decimal points. Then add or subtract. Add a 0 as a place holder if necessary.

Example: 22 – 14.73 = ?
$$\begin{array}{r} 22.00 \\ -\ 14.73 \\ \hline 7.27 \end{array}$$

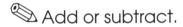 Add or subtract.

1.  $\begin{array}{r} 3.25 \\ +\ 1.89 \\ \hline \end{array}$

2.  $\begin{array}{r} 15.02 \\ -\ 8.86 \\ \hline \end{array}$

3.  $\begin{array}{r} 212.14 \\ +\ 96.28 \\ \hline \end{array}$

4.  $\begin{array}{r} 121.91 \\ 64.82 \\ +\ 71.63 \\ \hline \end{array}$

5.  $\begin{array}{r} 114.90 \\ -\ 86.92 \\ \hline \end{array}$

6.  600 + 81.3 + 10.42 = _____

7.  101.46 + 74.8 = _____

8.  50 – 4.19 = _____

9.  200 – 0.56 = _____

10. 743.9 – 57.13 = _____

11. Clay went to the movie with $20. He bought a ticket for $6.75. His popcorn and drink cost $5.40. How much money did he have left?  $ _____

12. A baseball player wanted new equipment. A bat cost $9.45; a ball cost $3.90; and a glove cost $24. How much did the new equipment cost in all? $ _____

- The chart shows the weights of several packages shipped to a book store.

| Package | Weight | Package | Weight |
|---------|--------|---------|--------|
| A | 33.9 kg | D | 123.2 kg |
| B | 40.4 kg | E | 94.6 kg |
| C | 26.05 kg | F | 85.8 kg |

1. Which two packages have a combined weight of 128.5 kg?

   _____

2. Which package is 8.8 kg heavier than Package F?

   _____

3. What is the weight difference between the heaviest and lightest

   packages?_____ kg

4. Which three packages have a combined weight of 100.35 kg?

   _____

5. What is the combined weight of the two lightest packages?

   _____ _____ kg

- Create an addition or subtraction problem about the packages in the chart.

   _____

   _____

 Ask one of your parents to explain how a car's odometer works. Record the odometer reading on a Monday and again 3 days later. How many miles did the car go? Make up decimal addition and subtraction problems based on the car's odometer readings.

# Multiplying Decimals by Whole Numbers

To multiply a decimal by a whole number, set up the problem like this:

$$1.8 \text{ ——— factor}$$
$$\underline{\times\ 6} \text{ ——— factor}$$

After multiplying, count the number of decimal places in the factors. Mark off the same number of decimal places in the product.

$$1.8 \quad \text{one decimal place in factor}$$
$$\underline{\times\ 6}$$
$$10.8 \quad \text{one decimal place in product}$$

✏️ Multiply.

1.  2.3
    x 4

2.  6.1
    x 7

3.  9.3
    x 2

4.  8.7 x 3 =

5.  7.1 x 5 =

6.  2.12
    x 9

7.  64.01
    x 22

8.  4.25 x 15 =

9.  10.15 x 11 =

10. A school bus travels 56.3 miles each day. How far will the bus travel in 5 days? _____ miles

11. Martin is making kites. For each kite, he needs 40.5 feet of string. How much string would he need for 7 kites? _____ feet

12. A case of juice holds 24 bottles. Each bottle holds 1.2 liters. What is the total amount of juice in the case? _____ liters

# Supplement and Answer Key to
## *Math and More*, Grade 5

**Note: This section can be easily removed from the workbook.**

### Hints for Using *Math and More*

- Provide a special place where young learners can work and learn. Keep basic supplies and materials (a dictionary, paper, pencils, colors, etc.) within easy reach of young hands.

- Work and learn together. Many activities in this book invite family members to join in the learning. Young learners respond when they know others are interested in what they are doing.

- Nurture a positive attitude about math. Make plenty of math objects and problems available for all family members. Discuss math concepts with young learners. Recognize and discuss the many uses of math in everyday life.

- Nurture a positive attitude about thinking. Extend the young learners' thinking by asking questions like the following: "Why do you think that is true?" "How did you come up with that answer?" "What else could you do with this information?" "Where have you seen something like this before?" Encourage young learners to ask themselves these kinds of questions, too.

- Challenge young learners to solve problems and find answers on their own. They can accomplish many things through persistence.

- Keep learning fun and challenging, but never frustrating. If something is too difficult, or if young learners become tired, put the activity away for another time.

- Try a positive incentive program. Reward young learners for completing lessons with stickers or some other appropriate treat. This book includes an "Achievement Award" for completing all the lessons. Celebrate successes, which come in many forms.

---

 **Other books in the ECS Home Study Collection™—**

|  Reading and More |  Language Arts and More | Math and More |
|---|---|---|
| Grade 1 | Grade 1 | Grade 1 |
| Grade 2 | Grade 2 | Grade 2 |
| Grade 3 | Grade 3 | Grade 3 |
| Grade 4 | Grade 4 | Grade 4 |
| Grade 5 | Grade 5 | Grade 6 |
| Grade 6 | Grade 6 | |

**Visit your local bookstore for these and other titles, or contact:**

ECS Learning Systems, Inc. • PO Box 791437 • San Antonio, TX 78279 • 1-800-688-3224

## Page 2

### Number Patterns

A number pattern is a series of numbers that follows a rule. The rule for the following pattern is "subtract 6." To find the next number in the pattern you must follow the rule.

39   33   27   21   15

The following pattern has two rules: "add 1, then multiply by 2." What is the next number in the pattern?

3   4   8   9   18   19   38   **39**

Write the missing numbers in each pattern.

1.  17  21  25  **29**  **33**  37  **41**
2.  6   5   8   7   10  9  **12**  **11**  14
3.  3   **9**   27  81  **243**
4.  2   5   8   8   11  **11**  14  14
5.  210  200  **190** **180**  170  160  **150** **140**
6.  1   4   9   **16**  25  36  **49**  **64**

Write the missing numbers in the pattern. Then write the pattern's rule.

1  3  6  8  **16** **18**  36  38

**add 2, then multiply by 2**

2

## Page 3

• Solve the word problem. Work in the space.

Sarah was helping her mother arrange fruit in baskets. Sarah placed 1 apple and 2 oranges in the first basket, 2 apples and 4 oranges in the second basket, and 4 apples and 8 oranges in the third basket. To continue the pattern, what combination of fruit would Sarah place in the fourth and fifth baskets?

> **In the fourth basket - 8 apples and 16 oranges**
>
> **In the fifth basket - 16 apples and 32 oranges**

• Choose 2 rules from the following list. Then build a pattern using those rules.

| multiply by 3 | divide by 3 | multiply by 4 |
| divide by 2 | subtract 7 | subtract 5 |
| add 9 | add 10 | add 8 |

**Answers will vary.**

Design a secret code that is based on a number pattern. Use the code to write a message to your parents. Can they "crack" the code?

3

## Page 4

### Translating Numbers

Numbers can be written as numerals or as words.

Write the numerals.

1. one million, three hundred forty-three thousand, one hundred one
   **1,343,101**
2. three million, four hundred five thousand, two hundred ten
   **3,405,210**
3. nine hundred thousand, four hundred twenty-one
   **900,421**
4. one million, fifty-two thousand, five hundred eighty-one
   **1,052,581**

Write the number words.

5. The new convention center cost the city $4,986,110.
   **four million, nine hundred eighty-six thousand, one hundred ten**
6. The bank loaned $368,900 to the company. **three hundred sixty-eight thousand, nine hundred**
7. Our town has a population of 8,321. **eight thousand, three hundred twenty-one**
8. The astronauts traveled 31,585 miles. **thirty-one thousand, five hundred eighty-five**

4

## Page 5

• You are planning a vacation to several different cities. Use a map to find the distance from your home to each of the following cities. Write each distance as a numeral and as words.

| City | Distance (Numeral) | Distance (Words) |
|------|-------------------|------------------|
| Chicago | | **Answers will vary.** |
| New York | | |
| San Francisco | | |
| New Orleans | | |

• If you traveled to each city and back, how many miles would you travel in all? Write the distance as a numeral and as words.

**Answers will vary.**

When do people usually write numbers as words? as numerals? Why? Talk to your mom or dad and find out when they write numbers as words.

5

## Page 6

### Place Value

We use 10 digits (1,2,3,4,5,6,7,8,9,0) to make every number. A digit's place, or position, shows its value in a number.

2  7  1  0  3  6  4 . 1  5

Write the answers.

1. What is the value of 2 in 2,980.764? **millions**
2. What is the value of 1 in 468,392.15? **tenths**
3. What is the value of 6 in 1,006.4787? **thousands**
4. What is the value of 9 in 56,901.46? **hundreds**
5. What is the value of 6 in 41.63? **tenths**
6. What is the value of 8 in 9,144.38? **hundredths**

Mark the correct answer with a check mark.

7. Which number has a 5 in the ones place and a 2 in the thousands place?
   - ☐ 6,327.915
   - ☑ 6,732.195
   - ☐ 6,273.159
   - ☐ 6,732.519

8. Which number has a 6 in the hundredths place and a 4 in the hundreds place?
   - ☐ 5,147.62
   - ☐ 5,147.26
   - ☑ 5,417.26
   - ☐ 5,417.62

6

## Page 7

• What is the value of 7 in each of the following numbers?

1. 7,140.06 **thousands**
2. 700,000 **hundred thousands**
3. 147.36 **ones**
4. 474.365 **ten thousands**
5. 1,000,000.07 **hundredths**
6. 1,000,000.7 **tenths**
7. 417.0 **ones**
8. 97,634.5 **thousands**

• Write a 5-digit number that has a 6 in the hundreds place.

**Answers will vary.**

Write a 6-digit number that has a 1 in the thousands place.

**Answers will vary.**

There is a 4 in the tenths place; a 6 in the thousands place; an 8 in the hundreds place; a 1 in the tens place; and a 3 in the ones place.

What is the number? **6,813.4**

Play this game with one of your parents. You will need 2 dice, paper, and pencil. Each person draws the following game board on paper: $ _ _ _ . _ _. The first player throws a die and writes the number shown in one of the game board's blanks. The second player does the same. Play continues until both players have filled in their game boards. Player with the greater amount wins the round. Play 10 rounds.

7

## Page 8

### Rounding

Rounding is one way to estimate or to know about how many. Look at the examples.

Round 315 to the nearest hundred.

To round to the nearest hundred, look at the tens digit. It is less than 5. The hundreds digit stays at 3 and the other digits are changed to 0. 315 rounded to the nearest hundred is 300.

Round 365 to the nearest hundred.

Look at the tens digit. It is greater than 5. Add 1 to the hundreds place. 365 rounded to the nearest hundred is 400.

Round to the nearest thousand.

1. 6,713 **7,000**
2. 1,010 **1,000**
3. 5,632 **6,000**
4. 36,417 **36,000**
5. 110,900 **111,000**
6. 111,056 **111,000**

Round to the nearest ten thousand.

7. 89,164 **90,000**
8. 76,410 **80,000**
9. 81,968 **80,000**
10. 67,000 **70,000**
11. 78,094 **80,000**
12. 126,078 **130,000**

Round to the nearest hundred thousand.

13. 403,987 **400,000**
14. 391,400 **400,000**
15. 1,201,933 **1,200,000**
16. 2,960,814 **3,000,000**

8

## Page 9

• Look at the population chart. Complete the chart by rounding each population to the nearest million.

| State | Population | Rounded Population |
|-------|-----------|--------------------|
| Alabama | 3,893,888 | **4,000,000** |
| California | 23,667,565 | **24,000,000** |
| Connecticut | 3,107,576 | **3,000,000** |
| Hawaii | 964,691 | **1,000,000** |
| Illinois | 11,426,518 | **11,000,000** |
| Minnesota | 4,075,970 | **4,000,000** |
| New Mexico | 1,302,981 | **1,000,000** |
| Texas | 14,229,288 | **14,000,000** |

Which states have about 4 times as many people as New Mexico?

**Alabama and Minnesota**

Which state has about the same number of people as Hawaii?

**New Mexico**

Ask your mom or dad to explain when they use rounding. Can you think of other times when rounding is a good way to estimate?

9

## Page 10

### Review

Solve each problem and circle the letter that matches a correct response. Unscramble the circled letters to find the name of a large city in the United States.

1. 6   16   26   **36**   46
2. 3   9   10   30   31   **93**   94
3. 4   **9**   16   25   36
4. 4   6   5   7   6   **8**   7
5. **101**   111   121   131   141
6. 1   3   3   5   5   **7**
7. 6   9   12   **15**   18   21
8. 4   8   12   16   **20**   24
9. 1   8   **27**   64   125
10. 1   4   3   12   11   **44**   43

| 101 A | 7 O | 36 L | 24 T | E | H | S | 91 U | 93 G | M | N | C | E | S | 15 Y | 27 O | 80 G |

**Los Angeles**

10

Answer each problem. Then add all the answers together. If you have answered correctly, the sum of the answers will be 1,000,000.

1. Write three hundred ten thousand, two hundred fifteen as a numeral. **310,215**

2. Write twenty-seven thousand, two hundred as a numeral. **27,200**

3. Which number has a 6 in the hundreds place: 126,120 or 121,620? **121,620**

4. Which number has a 1 in the ten thousands place: 381,452 or 314,548? **314,548**

5. Round 117,461 to the nearest thousand. **117,000**

6. Round 56,096 to the nearest hundred. **56,100**

7. Round 946 to the nearest thousand. **1,000**

8. Round 21,416 to the nearest ten. **21,420**

9. Round 27,010 to the nearest ten thousand. **30,000**

10. Write the number that has a 7 in the ones place, an 8 in the hundreds place, and a 9 in the tens place. **897**

---

## Number Lines: Decimals

A number line shows numbers in order from least to greatest. A number line lets you compare numbers. The following number line shows numbers from 0 to 1.0.

The number line shows that 0.2 is less 0.8. In math, you write it this way: 0.2 < 0.8.

Fill in the missing numbers on the number lines.

1.  **2.0 2.5   4.0**

2.  **0.6  1.0 1.2 1.6**

Write the symbol < (less than) or > (greater than) to make each of the following number sentences true.

3. 0.5 (<) 1.0
4. 0.4 (>) 0
5. 3.5 (>) 3.0
6. 1.2 (<) 1.4

7. 0.6 (>) 0.2
8. 1.0 (>) 0.5
9. 0.8 (<) 1.0
10. 1.6 (>) 1.2

---

* The chart shows the average rainfall in several cities during January and February.

| | |
|---|---|
| ✓ Dallas, Texas | 1.8 inches |
| ✗ Chicago, Illinois | 1.5 inches |
| ✚ Boise, Idaho | 1.4 inches |
| ✦ Helena, Montana | 0.6 inches |
| ▦ Minneapolis, Minnesota | 0.9 inches |
| ♥ Oklahoma City, Oklahoma | 1.2 inches |
| ➜ Phoenix, Arizona | 0.7 inches |
| ✦ Reno, Nevada | 1.1 inches |

Place the rainfall amounts on the number line. Write the city's symbol above the correct amount of rainfall.

**0   0.6 0.7   0.9  1.11.2  1.41.5   1.8   2**

Find at least 10 canned foods that have different weights (use metric weight). Arrange the items from least to greatest weight. Can you make a number line that shows the weight of each can?

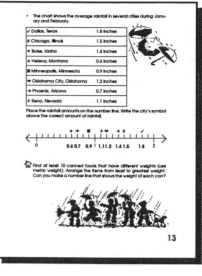

---

## Comparing Decimals

To compare decimals, compare the digits in the tenths place first. If the digits in the tenths place are the same, compare the digits in the hundredths place.

0.5 > 0.1    Compare the tenths.
0.54 > 0.51    Compare the hundredths.

Circle the decimal that is greater.

1. (0.15)  0.06
2. 0.6  (0.7)
3. 0.11  (0.12)
4. 0.48  (0.58)
5. (0.9)  0.89
6. (0.2)  0.19
7. 0.31  (0.33)
8. (0.7)  0.68

Write the symbol < (less than) or > (greater than) to make the following number sentences true.

9. 0.12 (<) 0.15
10. 0.7 (>) 0.65
11. 0.25 (>) 0.2
12. 0.36 (<) 0.41

13. 0.93 (>) 0.91
14. 0.47 (<) 0.51
15. 0.03 (<) 0.12
16. 0.09 (>) 0.08

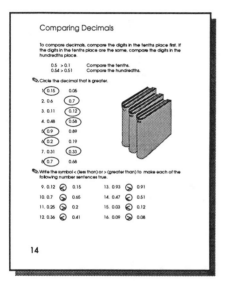

---

* Mrs. Davidson, the librarian, has several new books to shelf. Each book has a special number that includes a decimal. Mrs. Davidson must place the books on the shelf from least to greatest, according to their numbers. Can you help her? Number the books in the correct order.

| | | | |
|---|---|---|---|
| 7 | 5 | 4 | 3 |
| 301.12 | 212.13 | 151.12 | 151.09 |
| 1 | 12 | 11 | 10 |
| 116.4 | 911.24 | 800.56 | 792.44 |
| 8 | 6 | 2 | 9 |
| 331.56 | 212.2 | 116.42 | 664.81 |

Visit a library with one of your parents. Ask the librarian about the Dewey Decimal System and how it is used.

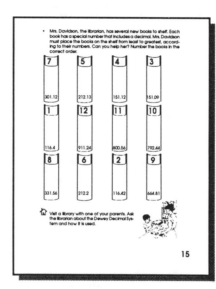

---

## Fractions

Fractions are numbers that describe parts of a whole. Look at the example.

$\frac{1}{3}$ of the box is shaded.

(numerator over denominator)

A fraction has a denominator and a numerator. The denominator tells the total number of equal pieces in the whole. The numerator tells how many of the equal pieces are in the number. Look at the example again. It was divided into 3 equal sections. Only 1 section has been shaded. The numerator is 1.

Divide and shade each box to show the fraction.

$\frac{2}{4}$     $\frac{3}{8}$

$\frac{2}{3}$     $\frac{3}{10}$

$\frac{3}{5}$     $\frac{3}{4}$

$\frac{1}{6}$     $\frac{5}{8}$

---

* Look at the chart and answer the questions.

### Neighborhood Pets

| | Dogs | Cats | Hamsters | Fish |
|---|---|---|---|---|
| McGuire Family | 2 | 0 | 1 | 0 |
| Jackson Family | 1 | 1 | 0 | 0 |
| Evans Family | 2 | 2 | 1 | 0 |
| Martinez Family | 0 | 0 | 2 | 5 |
| Wong Family | 1 | 1 | 1 | 1 |

1. What fraction of the McGuires' pets are dogs? **2/3**
2. What fraction of the Wongs' pets are fish? **1/4**
3. What fraction of the Martinez family's pets are hamsters? **2/7**
4. What fraction of the Evan family's pets are cats? **2/5**
5. What fraction of the Jacksons' pets are dogs? **1/2**
6. Which family owns 2/5 of all the hamsters? **Martinez**
7. Which family owns 1/6 of all the fish? **Wong**
8. What fraction of all the families own dogs? **4/5**
9. What fraction of all the families own cats? **3/5**
10. What fraction of all the families own hamsters? **4/5**
11. What fraction of all the families own fish? **2/5**
12. The Martinez family owns the greatest number of pets. What fraction of all the neighborhood pets do they own? **7/21**

Make a neighborhood pet chart like the one above, but record the pets that some of your neighbors own. Write the fractions that describe how many of your neighbors' pets are dogs, cats, hamsters, or fish. Ask your parents to help you.

**(1/3)**

---

## Comparing Fractions

To compare fractions with the same denominator, look at the numerator.

$$\frac{1}{3} < \frac{2}{3}$$

To compare fractions with different denominator, you must rewrite the fractions so that they have common denominators.

$$\frac{3}{4} \; \bigcirc \; \frac{1}{2}$$

Ask: How many fourths equal $\frac{1}{2}$ ?

Express $\frac{1}{2}$ in fourths: $\frac{1}{2} = \frac{2}{2} = \frac{2}{4}$

Compare the fractions: $\frac{3}{4} > \frac{2}{4}$

Write the symbol < (less than), > (greater than), or = (equals) to make each of the following number sentences true.

1. $\frac{2}{5}$ (<) $\frac{3}{5}$
2. $\frac{1}{4}$ (<) $\frac{2}{4}$
3. $\frac{4}{10}$ (=) $\frac{2}{5}$
4. $\frac{2}{3}$ (>) $\frac{3}{10}$

5. $\frac{2}{4}$ (<) $\frac{6}{12}$
6. $\frac{3}{8}$ (>) $\frac{1}{4}$
7. $\frac{4}{5}$ (>) $\frac{1}{2}$
8. $\frac{4}{15}$ (<) $\frac{3}{5}$

9. $\frac{1}{2}$ (>) $\frac{2}{6}$
10. $\frac{4}{8}$ (>) $\frac{1}{4}$
11. $\frac{2}{3}$ (>) $\frac{7}{12}$
12. $\frac{1}{3}$ (<) $\frac{3}{7}$

---

* Greg, Teddy, Mike, and Jimmy each bought a candy bar at the movie theater. Each candy bar was the same size, but each one had a different number of sections. Look at the chart to find out more about the boys' candy bars and how much they ate. Then answer the questions.

| | Total Number of Sections | Sections Eaten |
|---|---|---|
| Greg | 6 | 2 |
| Teddy | 3 | 2 |
| Mike | 2 | 1 |
| Jimmy | 4 | 1 |

1. What fraction of his candy bar did each boy eat?
Greg **2/6**  Teddy **2/3**  Mike **1/2**  Jimmy **1/4**
2. Which boy ate the most candy? **Teddy**
3. Which boy ate the least candy? **Jimmy**
4. True or False: Greg ate more candy than Jimmy. **True**
5. True or False: Mike ate more candy than Greg. **True**
6. True or False: Teddy ate more candy than Mike. **True**
7. True or False: Greg ate more candy than Mike. **False**
8. True or False: Jimmy ate more candy than Teddy. **False**

Ask your mom or dad to give you some plastic cups and containers of different sizes. Use the cups and containers to work with fractions. For example, can you figure out which cup or container is about 1/3 the size of another? Can you figure out which cup or container is about 1/2 the size of another? Explain your work to your mom or dad.

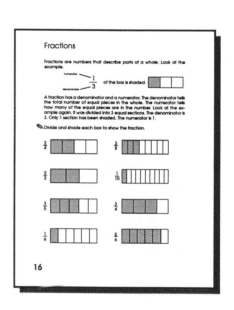

## Page 20 — Writing Fractions in Lowest Terms

The fraction 1/3 is in lowest terms. Its numerator and denominator can only be divided by 1.

The fraction 2/4 is not in lowest terms. Its numerator and denominator can be divided by 1 and by 2. Look at the example.

$$\frac{2}{4} \div \frac{2}{2} = \frac{1}{2}$$

A fraction is in lowest terms when the numerator and denominator can only be divided by 1.

Circle the fractions that are written in lowest terms.

1. $\frac{2}{6}$  2. $\frac{2}{6}$  3. $\frac{2}{10}$  4. $\frac{4}{9}$

5. $\frac{3}{8}$  6. $\frac{7}{9}$  7. $\frac{3}{6}$  8. $\frac{6}{12}$

9. $\frac{4}{8}$  10. $\frac{3}{8}$  11. $\frac{4}{9}$  12. $\frac{3}{8}$

Rewrite each fraction in lowest terms.

13. $\frac{4}{12} = \frac{1}{3}$  14. $\frac{6}{12} = \frac{1}{2}$  15. $\frac{4}{6} = \frac{2}{3}$  16. $\frac{6}{9} = \frac{2}{3}$

17. $\frac{5}{10} = \frac{1}{2}$  18. $\frac{2}{10} = \frac{1}{5}$  19. $\frac{3}{12} = \frac{1}{4}$  20. $\frac{6}{15} = \frac{2}{5}$

21. $\frac{2}{8} = \frac{1}{4}$  22. $\frac{3}{9} = \frac{1}{3}$  23. $\frac{10}{15} = \frac{2}{3}$  24. $\frac{6}{8} = \frac{3}{4}$

20

## Page 21

- Barbara's friend gave her the recipe for a great cake, but Barbara didn't have the same kind of measuring cups and spoons as her friend. Help Barbara by figuring out which of her measuring cups and spoons she should use.

Ingredients:

3/12 cup of butter          6/9 cup of white sugar
5/20 cup of milk            6/8 teaspoon of baking powder
2/4 cup of nuts             6/24 teaspoon of salt
3/9 cup of brown sugar      2 and 6/24 cups of flour

Barbara's measuring cups and spoons:

1/4 cup, 1/3 cup, 1/2 cup, 2/3 cup, 3/4 cup, 1 cup,
1/4 teaspoon, 1/2 teaspoon, 3/4 teaspoon, 1 teaspoon

Write the measuring cup or spoon that Barbara should use to measure:

the butter __1/4 cup__
the milk __1/4 cup__
the nuts __1/2 cup__
the brown sugar __1/3 cup__
the white sugar __2/3 cup__
the baking powder __3/4 teaspoon__
the salt __1/4 teaspoon__
the flour __1 cup and 1/4 cup__

🏠 Use a set of kitchen measuring cups and measuring spoons to learn more about fractions. For example, how many different ways can you measure 1/2 cup? How many different ways can you measure 1/4 cup? How many different ways can you measure 1/2 teaspoon? Ask your mom or dad to help you.

21

## Page 22 — Review

Compare each pair of decimals. Circle the letter written under the greater decimal in each pair. Write the circled letters on the line. Unscramble the letters to spell the name of a continent.

1. 0.45  0.4       2. 2.2  2.15
   (R)   S            (U)  T

3. 0.09  0.11      4. 0.56  0.55
   M    (L)           (S)   N

5. 1.06  1.16      6. 2.22  2.06
   E    (A)           (A)   P

7. 0.06  0.07      8. 0.1  0.09
   H    (T)           (I)  E

9. 3.0  3.01
   U   (A)

__RULSAATIA__
__Australia__

22

## Page 23

None of the following fractions are in lowest terms. Write each fraction on the chart under the fraction that expresses each one in lowest terms.

$\frac{2}{6}$  $\frac{3}{9}$  $\frac{6}{9}$  $\frac{4}{6}$  $\frac{2}{4}$  $\frac{3}{12}$

$\frac{5}{10}$  $\frac{4}{12}$  $\frac{6}{9}$  $\frac{12}{16}$  $\frac{2}{8}$  $\frac{6}{15}$

$\frac{15}{20}$  $\frac{9}{12}$  $\frac{3}{12}$  $\frac{2}{10}$

| $\frac{1}{2}$ | $\frac{1}{3}$ | $\frac{2}{3}$ | $\frac{1}{4}$ | $\frac{3}{4}$ | $\frac{1}{5}$ | $\frac{2}{5}$ |
|---|---|---|---|---|---|---|
| 6/12 | 2/6 | 4/6 | 2/8 | 15/20 | 2/10 | 6/15 |
| 2/4 | 3/9 | 6/9 | 3/12 | 12/16 | | |
| 5/10 | 4/12 | | | | | |
| 3/6 | | | 9/12 | | | |

Compare each set of fractions. Circle the letter under the greater fraction to find the name of a city in the United States.

1. $\frac{2}{5}$ $\frac{3}{7}$      2. $\frac{2}{3}$ $\frac{3}{10}$     3. $\frac{1}{2}$ $\frac{2}{6}$
   N  (I)           (M)  U           (A)  E

4. $\frac{1}{4}$ $\frac{3}{5}$      5. $\frac{3}{7}$ $\frac{2}{7}$
   P  (I)           T  (M)

__Miami__

23

## Page 24 — Operations Review

You should know how to add, subtract, multiply, and divide whole numbers.

Add or subtract.

1.  864      2.  1099      3.  4710      4.  5148
   + 738        + 872       - 1852       + 4894
   1,602        1,971       2,858        10,042

5.  907      6.  7610      7.  999       8.  3066
   - 159       - 4607       + 101        - 1847
   748         2,903        1,100        1,219

Multiply or divide.

9.  73       10.  807      11.  600      12.  971
   X 29         X 34         X 10         X 69
   2,117        27,438       6,000        66,999

13. 7)806 = 115r1   14. 3)7184 = 2,394r2   15. 14)7002 = 500r2

16. 23)6946 = 302   17. 16)1000 = 62r8   18. 4)4172 = 1,043

24

## Page 25

- Solve the following word problems.

1. Carrie's family took a trip. On the first day they drove 120 km. On the second day they drove 153 km, and on the third day they drove 178 km. How many kilometers did they drive in 3 days?

   __451__ km

2. Chris practiced his trumpet for 30 minutes each day. How many minutes did he practice in 2 weeks?

   __420__ minutes

3. A movie theater holds 986 seats. If 338 seats were empty during the first show, how many tickets had been sold?

   __648__ tickets

4. A museum had 848 visitors to a special exhibit. If visitors toured the exhibit in groups of 16, how many groups took the tour?

   __53__ groups

- Place the correct operation signs (+, -, x, ÷) for each problem.

5. 92 (x) 86 = 7912
6. 462 (+) 21 = 22
7. 569 (+) 263 - 129 = 703
8. 500 (-) 234 (+) 697 = 963
9. 42 (x) 16 (+) 6 = 112
10. 2236 (+) 52 (x) 21 = 903

🏠 Ask your parents how they use addition, subtraction, multiplication, and division each day.

25

## Page 26 — Adding & Subtracting Decimals

To add or subtract decimals, first line up the decimal points. Then add or subtract. Add a 0 as a place holder if necessary.

Example: 22 - 14.73 = ?        22.00
                               - 14.73
                                  7.27

Add or subtract.

1.  3.25      2.  15.02      3.  212.14
   + 1.89        - 8.86        + 96.28
   5.14          6.16         308.42

4.  121.91     5.  114.90
     64.82         - 86.92
   + 71.63         27.98
   258.36

6. 600 + 81.3 + 10.42 = __691.72__

7. 101.46 + 74.8 = __176.26__

8. 50 - 4.19 = __45.81__

9. 200 - 0.56 = __199.44__

10. 743.9 - 57.13 = __686.77__

11. Clay went to the movie with $20. He bought a ticket for $6.75. His popcorn and drink cost $5.40. How much money did he have left? $ __7.85__

12. A baseball player wanted new equipment. A bat cost $9.45; a ball cost $3.90; and a glove cost $24. How much did the new equipment cost in all? $ __37.35__

26

## Page 27

- The chart shows the weights of several packages shipped to a book store.

| Package | Weight | Package | Weight |
|---|---|---|---|
| A | 33.9 kg | D | 123.2 kg |
| B | 40.4 kg | E | 94.6 kg |
| C | 26.05 kg | F | 85.8 kg |

1. Which two packages have a combined weight of 128.5 kg?
   __A & E__

2. Which package is 8.8 kg heavier than Package F?
   __E__

3. What is the weight difference between the heaviest and lightest packages? __97.15__ kg

4. Which three packages have a combined weight of 100.35 kg?
   __A, B, & C__

5. What is the combined weight of the two lightest packages?
   __59.95__ kg

- Create an addition or subtraction problem about the packages in the chart.
   __Answers will vary.__

🏠 Ask one of your parents to explain how a car's odometer works. Record the odometer reading on a Monday and again 3 days later. How many miles did the car go? Make up decimal addition and subtraction problems based on the car's odometer readings.

27

## Page 28 — Multiplying Decimals by Whole Numbers

To multiply a decimal by a whole number, set up the problem like this:

       1.8 ← factor
     X 6 ← factor

After multiplying, count the number of decimal places in the factors. Mark off the same number of decimal places in the product.

       1.8 ← one decimal place in factor
     X 6
      10.8 ← one decimal place in product

Multiply.

1.  2.3      2.  6.1      3.  9.3      4. 8.7 X 3 = __26.1__
   X 4          X 7          X 2
   9.2          42.7        18.6       5. 7.1 X 5 = __35.5__

6.  2.12     7.  64.01
   X 9          X 22
   19.08       1408.22

8. 4.25 x 15 = __63.75__

9. 10.15 x 11 = __111.65__

10. A school bus travels 56.3 miles each day. How far will the bus travel in 5 days? __281.5__ miles

11. Martin is making kites. For each kite, he needs 40.5 feet of string. How much string would he need for 7 kites? __283.5__ feet

12. A case of juice holds 24 bottles. Each bottle holds 1.2 liters. What is the total amount of juice in the case? __28.8__ liters

28

- Chef Pierre made 4 cakes for a party. Each cake was the same size and same shape, but Chef Pierre cut each one differently. The pictures show how each cake was cut. Use the pictures to answer the questions. Express each answer in lowest terms.

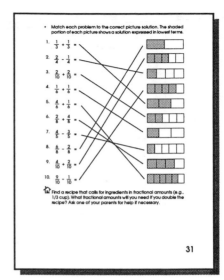

Cake 1 | A | B |
Cake 2 | C | D | E |
Cake 3 | F | G | H | I |
Cake 4 | J | K | L | M | N |

What fraction would equal each of the following? Express each fraction in lowest terms.

1. A + C = $\frac{5}{6}$   2. F + J = $\frac{9}{20}$

3. (C + D) - G = $\frac{5}{12}$   4. D - M = $\frac{2}{15}$

5. (J + K + L + M) - (F + G) = $\frac{3}{10}$   (B + F) - (M + N) = $\frac{7}{20}$

- Create an addition and subtraction problem about Chef Pierre's cakes. **Answers will vary.**

- Write the missing numerators.

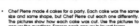

1. $\frac{1}{2} - \frac{\boxed{2}}{4} = \frac{5}{6}$   2. $\frac{7}{8} - \frac{\boxed{3}}{4} = \frac{1}{8}$   3. $\frac{\boxed{1}}{2} + \frac{9}{10} = \frac{9}{10}$

4. $\frac{1}{2} - \frac{\boxed{2}}{4} = 1$   5. $\frac{1}{8} + \frac{\boxed{3}}{4} = \frac{7}{16}$   6. $\frac{1}{2} - \frac{\boxed{2}}{3} = \frac{5}{9}$

7. $\frac{7}{10} - \frac{\boxed{3}}{4} = 1$   8. $\frac{1}{4} - \frac{\boxed{1}}{12} = 1$   9. $\frac{1}{2} - \frac{\boxed{1}}{3} = \frac{5}{6}$

 Talk to several adults and ask them how they use fractions in their work.

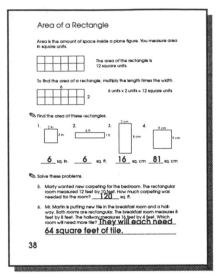

## Area of a Rectangle

Area is the amount of space inside a plane figure. You measure area in square units.

The area of the rectangle is 12 square units.

To find the area of a rectangle, multiply the length times the width.

6 units x 2 units = 12 square units

✏ Find the area of these rectangles.

1. 2 in. / 3 in.   2. 6 ft.   3. 2 cm / 8 cm   4. 9 cm

   __6__ sq. in.   __6__ sq. ft.   __16__ sq. cm   __81__ sq. cm

✏ Solve these problems.

5. Marty wanted new carpeting for the bedroom. The rectangular room measured 12 feet by 10 feet. How much carpeting was needed for the room? __120__ sq. ft.

6. Mr. Martin is putting new tile in the breakfast room and a hallway. Both rooms are rectangular. The breakfast room measures 8 feet by 8 feet. The hallway measures 16 feet by 4 feet. Which room will need more tile? **They will each need 64 square feet of tile.**

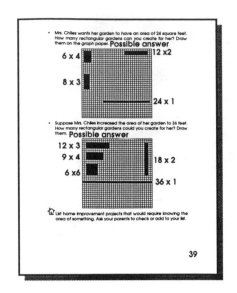

• Mrs. Chiles wants her garden to have an area of 24 square feet. How many rectangular gardens can you create for her? Draw them on the graph paper. **Possible answer**

6 x 4     12 x 2

8 x 3     24 x 1

• Suppose Mrs. Chiles increased the area of her garden to 36 feet. How many rectangular gardens could you create for her? Draw them. **Possible answer**

12 x 3     18 x 2

9 x 4

6 x 6     36 x 1

⌂ List home improvement projects that would require knowing the area of something. Ask your parents to check or add to your list.

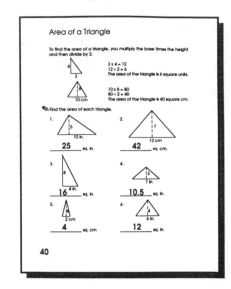

## Area of a Triangle

To find the area of a triangle, you multiply the base times the height and then divide by 2.

3 x 4 = 12
12 ÷ 2 = 6
The area of the triangle is 6 square units.

10 x 8 = 80
80 ÷ 2 = 40
The area of the triangle is 40 square cm.

✏ Find the area of each triangle.

1. 5 / 10 in.     __25__ sq. in.
2. 7 / 12 cm     __42__ sq. cm
3. 8 / 4 in.     __16__ sq. in.
4. 3 / 7 in.     __10.5__ sq. in.
5. 4 / 2 cm     __4__ sq. cm
6. 4 / 6 in.     __12__ sq. in.

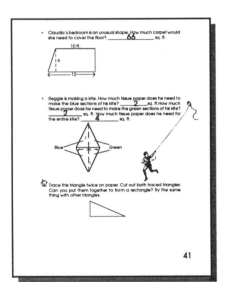

• Claudia's bedroom is an unusual shape. How much carpet would she need to cover the floor? __66__ sq. ft.

10 ft. / 6 / 12

• Reggie is making a kite. How much tissue paper does he need to make the blue sections of his kite? __2__ sq. ft. How much tissue paper does he need to make the green sections of his kite? __2__ sq. ft. How much tissue paper does he need for the entire kite? __4__ sq. ft.

Blue     Green

⌂ Trace this triangle twice on paper. Cut out both traced triangles. Can you put them together to form a rectangle? Try the same thing with other triangles.

## Three-Dimensional Figures

Polyhedrons are three-dimensional figures. Each face of a polyhedron is a polygon.

Cube     Rectangular Prism

Some three-dimensional figures are not polyhedrons.

Cylinder     Sphere

✏ Match each picture to the correct name.

1. rectangular prism
2. triangular pyramid
3. sphere
4. cube
5. square pyramid
6. triangular prism
7. cone
8. cylinder

• Find "real-life" examples for each three-dimensional figure on the chart. For example, a block is a rectangular prism.

| Rectangular prism | | | |
|---|---|---|---|
| Cone | | | |
| Sphere | | | |
| Cylinder | | | |
| Triangular pyramid | **Answers will vary.** | | |
| Cube | | | |
| Triangular prism | | | |
| Rectangular pyramid | | | |
| Square pyramid | | | |

⌂ Buy or make modeling clay. Make three-dimensional figures from the clay. Ask your parents to work with you.

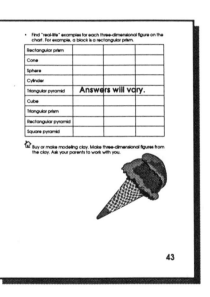

## Volume

Volume is the amount of space within a three-dimensional figure. You measure volume in cubic units. To find the volume of a cube or a rectangular prism, multiply the length times the width, times the height.

3 x 2 x 4 = 24 cubic units

✏ Find the volume of each three-dimensional figure.

1. 4 / 4 cm     __64__ cu. cm
2. 5 / 3 in.     __30__ cu. in.
3. 2 cm / 8     __16__ cu. cm
4. 2 / 2 in.     __8__ cu. in.

5. A cereal box is 11 inches tall, 5 inches wide, and 8 inches long. How much cereal can it hold? __440__ cu. in.

6. A bathtub is 6 feet long, 4 feet wide, and 1 foot tall. How much water could it hold? __24__ cu. ft.

• Find items that are rectangular prisms or cubes (e.g., cardboard box). Measure the height, length, and width of each item. Then determine the volume of each item.

| Item | Height | Length | Width | Volume |
|---|---|---|---|---|
| | | | | |
| | | **Answers will vary.** | | |
| | | | | |
| | | | | |

⌂ Which room in your home has the greatest volume? the least? Ask your parents to help you find the volume of each room in your house.

## Review

The chart shows the length and width of the playing area for different sports.

| Playing Area | Length | Width | Perimeter | Area |
|---|---|---|---|---|
| Football field | 300 ft. | 160 ft. | **920 ft.** | **48,000 sq. ft** |
| Basketball court | 94 ft. | 50 ft. | **288 ft.** | **4,700 sq. ft.** |
| Baseball diamond (infield) | 90 ft. | 90 ft. | **360 ft.** | **8,100 sq. ft.** |
| Soccer field | 100 m | 80 m | **360 ft.** | **8,000 sq. ft.** |

Find the perimeter and area for each playing area and record the answers on the chart.

Answer each question.

1. When it rains, workers often cover the infield of a baseball diamond with a plastic tarp. How large would the tarp need to be? __8,100__ sq. ft.

2. Jack's coach makes the football team run around the football field once at the end of each practice. How far do the players run? __920__

3. The basketball coach wants a new floor for the basketball court. How much flooring will he need to buy? __4,700__ sq. ft.

4. The school spirit squad wants to make a banner that will stretch completely around the soccer field. How large would the banner have to be? __360__ ft.

## Page 47

Match each picture with the correct three-dimensional figure.

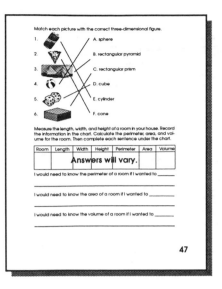

1. A. sphere
2. B. rectangular pyramid
3. C. rectangular prism
4. D. cube
5. E. cylinder
6. F. cone

Measure the length, width, and height of a room in your house. Record the information in the chart. Calculate the perimeter, area, and volume for the room. Then complete each sentence under the chart.

| Room | Length | Width | Height | Perimeter | Area | Volume |
|------|--------|-------|--------|-----------|------|--------|
| Answers will vary. | | | | | | |

I would need to know the perimeter of a room if I wanted to _____

I would need to know the area of a room if I wanted to _____

I would need to know the volume of a room if I wanted to _____

## Page 48

## Pictographs

Charts and graphs are an easy, convenient way to record, organize, and present information.

On a **pictograph** a picture or symbol represents a specific quantity. The **key** to a pictograph shows what each symbol or picture represents.

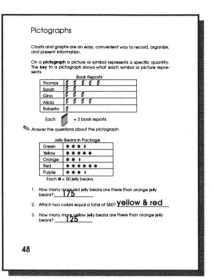

Book Reports

| Thomas | | | | | |
| Sarah | | |
| Gina | | | | |
| Alicia | | | | |
| Roberto | |

Each = 3 book reports.

Answer the questions about the pictograph.

Jelly Beans in Package

| Green | ● ● ● |
| Yellow | ● ● ● ● ● |
| Orange | ● ● ● |
| Red | ● ● ● ● ● ● |
| Purple | ● ● ● |

Each ● = 50 jelly beans.

1. How many more red jelly beans are there than orange jelly beans? **175**

2. Which two colors equal a total of 550? **yellow & red**

3. How many more yellow jelly beans are there than orange jelly beans? **125**

## Page 49

• Purchase a bag of candy that has candies of different colors. Design and make a pictograph that shows how many of each color are in the bag. Then write 3-5 questions that others could answer by using the pictograph.

**Answers will vary.**

_____

_____

_____

_____

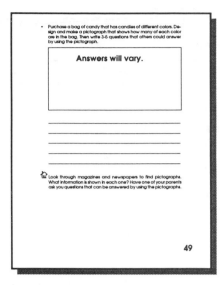 Look through magazines and newspapers to find pictographs. What information is shown in each one? Have one of your parents ask you questions that can be answered by using the pictographs.

## Page 50

## Bar Graphs

On a **bar graph** the length of each bar represents a certain quantity. The graph show the favorite soft drinks of the students in the class.

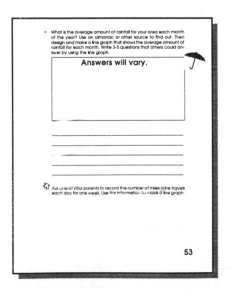

Favorite Soft Drinks

Answer the questions about the bar graph. The graph shows the favorite cafeteria lunches at the elementary school.

Favorite Lunches

1. How many more students like hamburgers than chicken? **50**

2. How many students like chicken or tacos? **175**

3. How many more students like tacos than chicken? **25**

## Page 51

• Ask at least 25 people to name their favorite cereal. Then design and make a bar graph that shows the results of the survey. Write 3-5 questions that others could answer by using the bar graph.

**Answers will vary.**

_____

_____

_____

_____

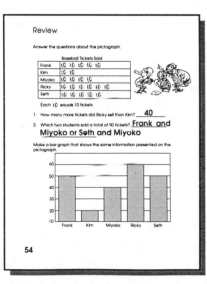 Ask your parents and other adults what kind of information they have seen presented on bar graphs. Look through some of your textbooks. Which books have bar graphs? What kind of information is presented on the graphs?

## Page 52

## Line Graphs

On a **line graph** the position of a line on a grid or chart represents a certain quantity. A line graph can also show changes in amounts over time.

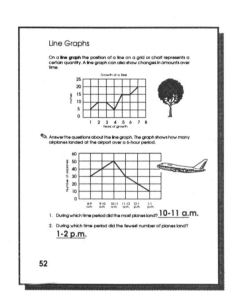

Growth of a tree

Answer the questions about the line graph. The graph shows how many airplanes landed at the airport over a 6-hour period.

1. During which time period did the most planes land? **10-11 a.m.**

2. During which time period did the fewest number of planes land? **1-2 p.m.**

## Page 53

• What is the average amount of rainfall for your area each month of the year? Use an almanac or other source to find out. Then design and make a line graph that shows the average amount of rainfall for each month. Write 3-5 questions that others could answer by using the line graph.

**Answers will vary.**

_____

_____

_____

_____

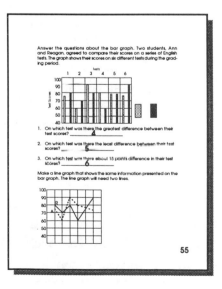 Ask one of your parents to record the number of miles (s)he travels each day for one week. Use this information to make a line graph.

## Page 54

## Review

Answer the questions about the pictograph.

Baseball Tickets Sold

| Frank | |
| Kim | |
| Miyoko | |
| Ricky | |
| Seth | |

Each = 10 tickets

1. How many more tickets did Ricky sell than Kim? **40**

2. Which two students sold a total of 90 tickets? **Frank and Miyoko or Seth and Miyoko**

Make a bar graph that shows the same information presented on the pictograph.

## Page 55

Answer the questions about the bar graph. Two students, Ann and Reagan, agreed to compare their scores on a series of English tests. The graph shows their scores on six different tests during the grading period.

1. On which test was there the greatest difference between their test scores? **4**

2. On which test was there the least difference between their test scores? **5**

3. On which test was there about 15 points difference in their test scores? **6**

Make a line graph that shows the same information presented on the bar graph. The line graph will need two lines.

This checklist highlights the math skills required for each activity. Review pages cover skills from preceding activities.

| Skills | Activities |
|---|---|
| Determine missing elements in patterns. | Number Patterns (pp. 2-3) |
| Translate whole numbers, name to numeral and numeral to name. | Translating Numbers (pp. 4-5) |
| Use whole number and decimal place value. | Place Value (pp. 6-7) |
| Round whole numbers (to nearest thousand, ten thousand, or hundred thousand). | Rounding (pp. 8-9) |
| Use number line representations of whole numbers and decimals. | Number Lines: Decimals (pp. 12-13) |
| Compare and order decimals. Use the mathematical symbols for less than and greater than. | Comparing Decimals (pp. 14-15) |
| Recognize fractions. | Fractions (pp. 16-17) |
| Compare fractions with same or different denominators. | Comparing Fractions (pp. 18-19) |
| Understand lowest terms. Reduce fractions to lowest terms. | Writing Fractions in Lowest Terms (pp. 20-21) |
| Add, subtract, multiply, and divide whole numbers. | Operations Practice (pp. 24-25) |
| Add and subtract decimals. Select strategies and solve word problems. | Adding & Subtracting Decimals (pp. 26-27) |
| Multiply whole numbers and decimals. Select strategies and solve word problems. | Multiplying Decimals by Whole Numbers (pp. 28-29) |
| Add and subtract fractions with the same denominator. Select strategies and solve word problems. | Adding & Subtracting Fractions with the Same Denominator (pp. 30-31) |
| Add and subtract fractions with different denominators. Select strategies and solve word problems. | Adding & Subtracting Fractions with Different Denominators (pp. 32-33) |
| Find perimeter with and without models. Select strategies and solve word problems. | Perimeter (pp. 36-37) |
| Find area of rectangles with and without models. Select strategies and solve word problems. | Area of a Rectangle (pp. 38-39) |
| Find area of triangles with models. | Area of a Triangle (pp. 40-41) |
| Recognize three-dimensional shapes and their properties. | Three-Dimensional Figures (pp. 42-43) |
| Find volume with and without models. Select strategies and solve word problems. | Volume (pp. 44-45) |
| Interpret charts and graphs. | Pictographs (pp. 48-49); Bar Graphs (pp. 50-51); Line Graphs (pp. 52-53) |

- - - ✂ - - - - - - - - - - - - - - - - - - - - - - - - - - - - - - - - - - - - - -

### The Home Study Team would like to recognize your child's achievement!

After your child successfully finishes this book, ask him/her to write a brief letter that explains what (s)he liked about the book and learned from completing the activities. Mail the child's letter and this completed coupon to: Home Study Team, ECS, PO Box 791437, San Antonio, TX 78279. **Include a legal-size, stamped, self-addressed envelope.** The Home Study Team will send:

- for the child—an embossed seal to attach to his/her Achievement Award
- for the parent—an informative pamphlet with more ideas for helping your child learn

Parent's Name _____

Address _____

City_____ State _____ Zip _____

Child's Name _____ Child's Age _____

Book Completed (circle one):     Reading          Language Arts          Math

Grade Level (circle one):      1      2      3      4      5      6

- A sports store sells the following items for ski trips.

| Ski gloves | $12.75 | Knit caps | $4.99 |
|------------|--------|-----------|-------|
| Lip balm | $1.39 | Snow boots | $27.39 |
| Sunglasses | $9.69 | Socks | $7.89 |

How much would the store charge for—

6 pairs of ski gloves? $ _____

a dozen lip balms? $ _____

9 pairs of snow boots? $ _____

5 pairs of sunglasses? $ _____

15 pairs of socks? $ _____

8 knit caps? $ _____

- This is a magic square. The sum of the numbers in each column, row, and diagonal is 15 (the "magic" sum). Multiply each number by 2.8 to create a new magic square. What is the new magic sum? _____

| 4 | 9 | 2 |
|---|---|---|
| 3 | 5 | 7 |
| 8 | 1 | 6 |

|   |   |   |
|---|---|---|
|   |   |   |
|   |   |   |
|   |   |   |

🏠 Use a grocery store ad and create multiplication problems that include decimals. Solve the problems. Ask your parents to check your work.

# Adding & Subtracting Fractions with the Same Denominator

To add fractions with the same denominator, add the numerators. Keep the same denominator.

$$\frac{1}{4} + \frac{2}{4} = \frac{3}{4}$$

To subtract fractions with the same denominator, subtract the numerators. Keep the same denominator.

$$\frac{5}{6} - \frac{4}{6} = \frac{1}{6}$$

✎ Add or subtract. Express answers in lowest terms.

1. $\dfrac{3}{5} + \dfrac{1}{5} =$     2. $\dfrac{2}{3} - \dfrac{1}{3} =$     3. $\dfrac{7}{8} - \dfrac{4}{8} =$

4. $\dfrac{5}{7} + \dfrac{1}{7} =$     5. $\dfrac{7}{10} + \dfrac{2}{10} =$     6. $\dfrac{4}{5} - \dfrac{3}{5} =$

7. $\dfrac{1}{7} + \dfrac{2}{7} + \dfrac{2}{7} =$     8. $\dfrac{1}{6} + \dfrac{1}{6} + \dfrac{1}{6} =$

9. $\dfrac{4}{8} - \dfrac{2}{8} =$     10. $\dfrac{3}{4} - \dfrac{1}{4} =$

11. Maria made 1 dozen cupcakes. Her brother ate 2 cupcakes and her father ate 1 cupcake. What fraction of the cupcakes did they eat? _____

    What fraction of the cupcakes was left? _____

12. Martin is working on a project for school. He needs 1/5 gallon of white paint and 2/5 gallon of green paint. How much paint does he need in all? _____ gallon

- Match each problem to the correct picture solution. The shaded portion of each picture shows a solution expressed in lowest terms.

1. $\dfrac{1}{3} + \dfrac{1}{3} =$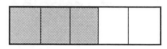

2. $\dfrac{2}{4} - \dfrac{1}{4} =$

3. $\dfrac{2}{10} + \dfrac{2}{10} =$

4. $\dfrac{1}{6} + \dfrac{1}{6} =$

5. $\dfrac{4}{6} + \dfrac{1}{6} =$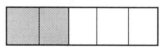

6. $\dfrac{2}{8} + \dfrac{4}{8} =$

7. $\dfrac{4}{5} - \dfrac{3}{5} =$

8. $\dfrac{6}{8} - \dfrac{2}{8} =$

9. $\dfrac{4}{10} + \dfrac{2}{10} =$

10. $\dfrac{9}{10} - \dfrac{1}{10} =$

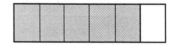

Find a recipe that calls for ingredients in fractional amounts (e.g., 1/3 cup). What fractional amounts will you need if you double the recipe? Ask one of your parents for help if necessary.

# Adding & Subtracting Fractions with Different Denominators

To add and subtract fractions with different denominators, you must first express both fractions with a common denominator.

$$\frac{1}{4} + \frac{1}{2} = ?$$     $$\frac{5}{8} - \frac{1}{4} = ?$$

$$\frac{1}{4} + \frac{2}{4} = \frac{3}{4}$$     $$\frac{5}{8} - \frac{2}{8} = \frac{3}{8}$$

✎ Add or subtract. Express all answers in lowest terms.

1. $\frac{1}{6} + \frac{1}{3} =$     2. $\frac{5}{8} + \frac{1}{4} =$     3. $\frac{7}{8} - \frac{1}{4} =$

4. $\frac{3}{10} + \frac{1}{5} =$     5. $\frac{7}{10} - \frac{1}{5} =$     6. $\frac{1}{2} - \frac{1}{8} =$

7. $\frac{1}{2} + \frac{1}{3} =$     8. $\frac{1}{2} - \frac{1}{3} =$     9. $\frac{1}{5} + \frac{1}{3} =$

10. $\frac{4}{5} - \frac{1}{3} =$

11. Mr. Frank bought candy for his students. His first class ate 1/5 of the candy. His second class ate 1/3 of the candy. What fraction of the candy did both classes eat? _____

12. Teresa is making dresses for her little sister's doll. She has 4/5 yard of ribbon. She must use 1/2 yard for one dress. How much ribbon will she have left? _____ yard

- Chef Pierre made 4 cakes for a party. Each cake was the same size and same shape, but Chef Pierre cut each one differently. The pictures show how each cake was cut. Use the pictures to answer the questions. Express each answer in lowest terms.

Cake 1

| A | B |
|---|---|

Cake 3

| F | G | H | I |
|---|---|---|---|

Cake 2

| C | D | E |
|---|---|---|

Cake 4

| J | K | L | M | N |
|---|---|---|---|---|

What fraction would equal each of the following? Express each fraction in lowest terms.

1.  A + C = _____

2.  F + J = _____

3.  (C + D) – G = _____

4.  D – M = _____

5.  (J + K + L + M) – (F + G) = _____

6.  (B + F) – (M + N) = _____

- Create an addition and subtraction problem about Chef Pierre's cakes.

- Write the missing numerators.

1.  $\dfrac{1}{6} + \dfrac{\square}{3} = \dfrac{5}{6}$

2.  $\dfrac{7}{8} - \dfrac{\square}{4} = \dfrac{1}{8}$

3.  $\dfrac{7}{10} + \dfrac{\square}{5} = \dfrac{9}{10}$

4.  $\dfrac{1}{2} - \dfrac{\square}{8} = \dfrac{1}{4}$

5.  $\dfrac{1}{16} + \dfrac{\square}{8} = \dfrac{7}{16}$

6.  $\dfrac{1}{3} + \dfrac{\square}{9} = \dfrac{5}{9}$

7.  $\dfrac{7}{10} - \dfrac{\square}{5} = \dfrac{1}{10}$

8.  $\dfrac{1}{4} - \dfrac{\square}{6} = \dfrac{1}{12}$

9.  $\dfrac{1}{2} + \dfrac{\square}{3} = \dfrac{5}{6}$

 Talk to several adults and ask them how they use fractions in their work.

# Review

A group of friends had summer jobs in their neighborhood. Use the clues to figure out how much each person earned during the summer.

★ John earned twice as much money as Carrie.

★ Bill earned $72.10.

★ Carrie earned $7.59 less than Bill.

★ Loni earned $4.35 less than John.

★ Jamie earned 4 times as much as Loni.

★ Crissy earned $42.78 more than Loni and Carrie did together.

★ Tom earned $54.13 less than Crissy.

John earned $ _____ .

Bill earned $ _____ .

Carrie earned $ _____ .

Loni earned $ _____ .

Jamie earned $ _____ .

Crissy earned $ _____ .

Tom earned $ _____ .

Solve each problem. Circle the letter under each correct answer. Unscramble the circled letters to find the answer to the riddle. All answers should be expressed in lowest terms.

1. $\dfrac{1}{4} + \dfrac{1}{4} =$

2. $\dfrac{1}{3} + \dfrac{1}{2} =$

3. $\dfrac{1}{8} + \dfrac{1}{4} =$

4. $\dfrac{9}{10} - \dfrac{1}{2} =$

5. $\dfrac{1}{5} + \dfrac{1}{10} =$

6. $\dfrac{7}{9} - \dfrac{2}{3} =$

7. $\dfrac{7}{8} - \dfrac{1}{4} =$

8. $\dfrac{5}{6} - \dfrac{1}{2} =$

9. $\dfrac{3}{4} + \dfrac{1}{8} =$

10. $\dfrac{7}{12} - \dfrac{1}{3} =$

Answers:

| $\dfrac{7}{8}$ | $\dfrac{3}{4}$ | $\dfrac{1}{2}$ | $\dfrac{5}{6}$ | $\dfrac{1}{8}$ | $\dfrac{3}{8}$ | $\dfrac{1}{5}$ | $\dfrac{2}{5}$ | $\dfrac{1}{3}$ | $\dfrac{5}{8}$ | $\dfrac{7}{10}$ | $\dfrac{1}{9}$ | $\dfrac{2}{3}$ | $\dfrac{1}{4}$ | $\dfrac{3}{10}$ | $\dfrac{1}{16}$ | $\dfrac{1}{7}$ |
|---|---|---|---|---|---|---|---|---|---|---|---|---|---|---|---|---|
| A | X | H | G | M | W | B | N | T | S | U | I | Y | O | N | K | L |

Which state would be the best place to open a laundromat?

"___ ___ ___ ___ ___ ___ ___" ___ ___ ___

# Perimeter

Perimeter is the distance around a polygon. Add the length of the sides to find the perimeter.

3 cm ╱ 5

$3 + 5 + 6 = 14$ cm

6

✎ Write the perimeter of each polygon.

1.

4        5 in.

3

_____ in.

2.

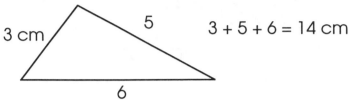

5 cm

5        5

5        5

5

_____ cm

3.

10 cm

10        10

10

_____ cm

4.

8 ft.

3

_____ ft.

5. David and Debbie want to put a fence around their rectangular garden that measures 10 feet by 6 feet. How much fencing do they need? _____ ft.

6. Shawna made a square tablecloth. She wanted to put lace trim around the edges. If one side of the tablecloth measured 5 feet, how many feet of lace did she need? _____ ft.

7. Tonya walks around the community park each day. How many miles does she walk? _____ mi.

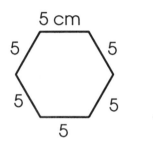

0.2        0.4 mi.

0.2        Community Park        0.15

0.4        0.25

- Mrs. Chiles has 8 feet of fence to put around a garden, but doesn't know what shape to make the garden. How many garden shapes can you create for her? Draw them on the graph paper. Each square equals 1 square foot.

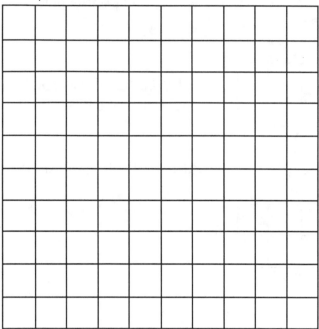

- Suppose Mrs. Chiles had 10 feet of fence. How many garden shapes could you create for her? Draw them. Each square equals 1 square foot.

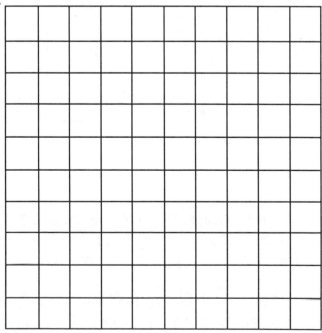

 List projects that would require knowing the perimeter of something. Ask your parents to check or add to your list.

# Area of a Rectangle

Area is the amount of space inside a plane figure. You measure area in square units.

The area of the rectangle is 12 square units.

To find the area of a rectangle, multiply the length times the width.

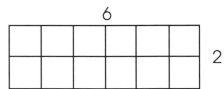

6 units x 2 units = 12 square units

✎ Find the area of these rectangles.

1.

2 in.
3

2.

6 ft.
1

3.
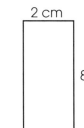
2 cm
8

4.
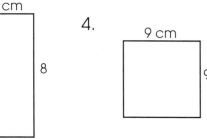
9 cm
9

_____ sq. in.     _____ sq. ft.     _____ sq. cm     _____ sq. cm

✎ Solve these problems.

5.  Marty wanted new carpeting for the bedroom. The rectangular room measured 12 feet by 10 feet. How much carpeting was needed for the room? _____ sq. ft.

6.  Mr. Martin is putting new tile in the breakfast room and a hallway. Both rooms are rectangular. The breakfast room measures 8 feet by 8 feet. The hallway measures 16 feet by 4 feet. Which room will need more tile? _____

- Mrs. Chiles wants her garden to have an area of 24 square feet. How many rectangular gardens can you create for her? Draw them on the graph paper. Each square equals 1 square foot.

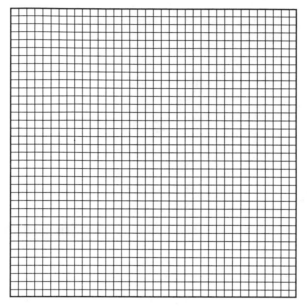

- Suppose Mrs. Chiles increased the area of her garden to 36 square feet. How many rectangular gardens could you create for her? Draw them. Each square equals 1 square foot.

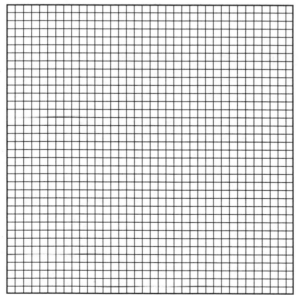

List home improvement projects that would require knowing the area of something. Ask your parents to check or add to your list.

# Area of a Triangle

To find the area of a triangle, you multiply the base times the height and then divide by 2.

4

3

$3 \times 4 = 12$
$12 \div 2 = 6$
The area of the triangle is 6 square units.

8

10 cm

$10 \times 8 = 80$
$80 \div 2 = 40$
The area of the triangle is 40 square cm.

✏️ Find the area of each triangle.

1.

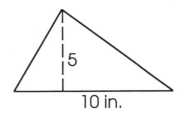

5

10 in.

_____ sq. in.

2.

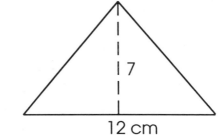

7

12 cm

_____ sq. cm

3.

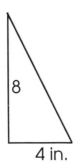

8

4 in.

_____ sq. in.

4.

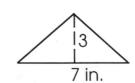

3

7 in.

_____ sq. in.

5.

4

2 cm

_____ sq. cm

6.

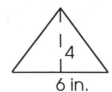

4

6 in.

_____ sq. in.

• Claudia's bedroom is an unusual shape. How much carpet would she need to cover the floor? _____ sq. ft.

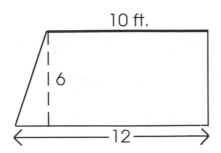

10 ft.

6

12

• Reggie is making a kite. How much tissue paper does he need to make the blue sections of his kite? _____ sq. ft. How much tissue paper does he need to make the green sections of his kite? _____ sq. ft. How much tissue paper does he need for the entire kite? _____ sq. ft.

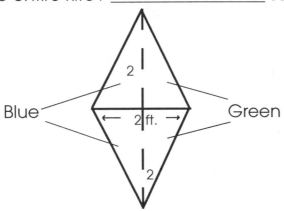

Blue          Green

2

2 ft.

2

🏠 Trace this triangle twice on paper. Cut out both traced triangles. Can you put them together to form a rectangle? Try the same thing with other triangles.

# Three-Dimensional Figures

Polyhedrons are three-dimensional figures. Each face of a polyhedron is a polygon.

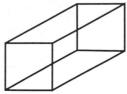

Cube          Rectangular Prism

Some three-dimensional figures are not polyhedrons.

Cylinder          Sphere

Match each picture to the correct name.

1.  rectangular prism

2.  triangular pyramid

3.  sphere

4.  cube

5.  square pyramid

6.  triangular prism

7.  cone

8.  cylinder

- Find "real-life" examples for each three-dimensional figure on the chart. For example, a block is a rectangular prism.

| Rectangular prism | | | |
|---|---|---|---|
| Cone | | | |
| Sphere | | | |
| Cylinder | | | |
| Triangular pyramid | | | |
| Cube | | | |
| Triangular prism | | | |
| Rectangular pyramid | | | |
| Square pyramid | | | |

Buy or make modeling clay. Make three-dimensional figures from the clay. Ask your parents to work with you.

# Volume

Volume is the amount of space within a three-dimensional figure. You measure volume in cubic units. To find the volume of a cube or a rectangular prism, multiply the length times the width, times the height.

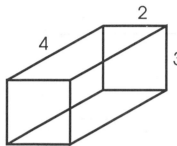

4 x 2 x 3 = 24 cubic units

✎ Find the volume of each three-dimensional figure.

1.
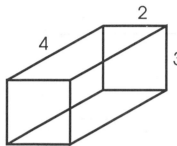

_____ cu. cm

2.
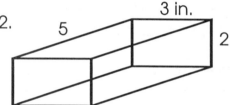

_____ cu. in.

3.
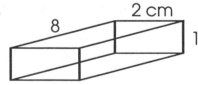

_____ cu. cm

4.
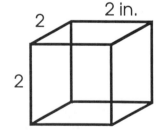

_____ cu. in.

5. A cereal box is 11 inches tall, 5 inches wide, and 8 inches long. How much cereal can it hold?_____ cu. in.

6. A bathtub is 6 feet long, 4 feet wide, and 1 foot tall. How much water could it hold?_____ cu. ft.

- Find items that are rectangular prisms or cubes (e.g., cardboard box). Measure the height, length, and width of each item. Then determine the volume of each item.

| Item | Height | Length | Width | Volume |
|------|--------|--------|-------|--------|
|      |        |        |       |        |
|      |        |        |       |        |
|      |        |        |       |        |
|      |        |        |       |        |
|      |        |        |       |        |
|      |        |        |       |        |
|      |        |        |       |        |
|      |        |        |       |        |
|      |        |        |       |        |

Which room in your home has the greatest volume? the least? Ask your parents to help you find the volume of each room in your home.

# Review

The chart shows the length and width of the playing area for different sports.

| Playing Area | Length | Width | Perimeter | Area |
|---|---|---|---|---|
| Football field | 300 ft. | 160 ft. | | |
| Basketball court | 94 ft. | 50 ft. | | |
| Baseball diamond (infield) | 90 ft. | 90 ft. | | |
| Soccer field | 100 m | 80 m | | |

Find the perimeter and area for each playing area and record the answers on the chart.

Answer each question.

1. When it rains, workers often cover the infield of a baseball diamond with a plastic tarp. How large would the tarp need to be? _____ sq. ft.

2. Jack's coach makes the football team run around the football field once at the end of each practice. How far do the players run? _____ ft.

3. The basketball coach wants a new floor for the basketball court. How much flooring will he need to buy? _____ sq. ft.

4. The school spirit squad wants to make a banner that will stretch completely around the soccer field. How large would the banner have to be? _____ m

Match each picture with the correct three-dimensional figure.

1.     A. sphere

2.     B. rectangular pyramid

3.     C. rectangular prism

4.     D. cube

5.     E. cylinder

6.     F. cone

Measure the length, width, and height of a room in your house. Record the information in the chart. Calculate the perimeter, area, and volume for the room. Then complete each sentence under the chart.

| Room | Length | Width | Height | Perimeter | Area | Volume |
|------|--------|-------|--------|-----------|------|--------|
|      |        |       |        |           |      |        |

I would need to know the perimeter of a room if I wanted to _____

_____

I would need to know the area of a room if I wanted to _____

_____

I would need to know the volume of a room if I wanted to _____

_____

# Pictographs

Charts and graphs are an easy, convenient way to record, organize, and present information.

On a pictograph a picture or symbol represents a specific quantity. The key to a pictograph shows what each symbol or picture represents.

## Book Reports

| Thomas | 📖 📖 📖 📖 📖 |
|---------|------------------|
| Sarah | 📖 📖 |
| Gina | 📖 📖 📖 |
| Alicia | 📖 📖 📖 📖 |
| Roberto | 📖 |

Each 📖 = 3 book reports.

✏️ Answer the questions about the pictograph.

## Jelly Beans in Package

| Green | ● ● ● ◗ |
|--------|-----------|
| Yellow | ● ● ● ● ● |
| Orange | ● ● ◗ |
| Red | ● ● ● ● ● ● |
| Purple | ● ● ● ◗ |

Each ● = 50 jelly beans.

1. How many more red jelly beans are there than orange jelly beans?_____

2. Which two colors equal a total of 550? _____

3. How many more yellow jelly beans are there than orange jelly beans? _____

- Purchase a bag of candy that has candies of different colors. Design and make a pictograph that shows how many of each color are in the bag. Then write 3-5 questions that others could answer by using the pictograph.

_____

_____

_____

_____

_____

Look through magazines and newspapers to find pictographs. What information is shown in each one? Have one of your parents ask you questions that can be answered by using the pictographs.

# Bar Graphs

On a bar graph the length of each bar represents a certain quantity. The graph shows the favorite soft drinks of the students in the class.

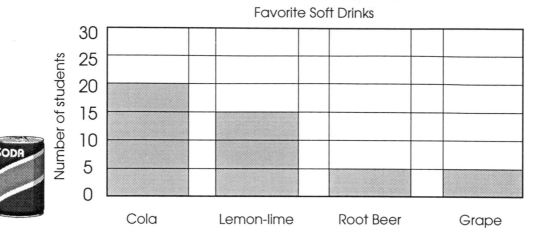

Favorite Soft Drinks

✎ Answer the questions about the bar graph. The graph shows the favorite cafeteria lunches at the elementary school.

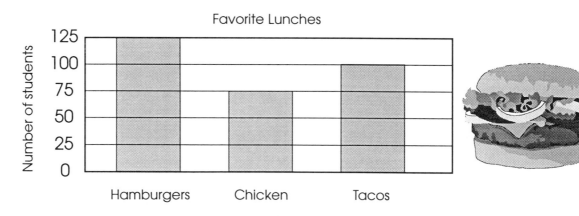

Favorite Lunches

1. How many more students like hamburgers than chicken? _____

2. How many students like chicken or tacos? _____

3. How many more students like tacos than chicken? _____

- Ask at least 25 people to name their favorite cereal. Then design and make a bar graph that shows the results of the survey. Write 3-5 questions that others could answer by using the bar graph.

Ask your parents and other adults what kind of information they have seen presented on bar graphs. Look through some of your textbooks. Which books have bar graphs? What kind of information is presented on the graphs?

# Line Graphs

On a line graph the position of a line on a grid or chart represents a certain quantity. A line graph can also show changes in amounts over time.

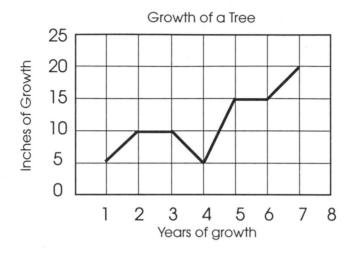

Growth of a Tree

Answer the questions about the line graph. The graph shows how many airplanes landed at the airport over a 6-hour period.

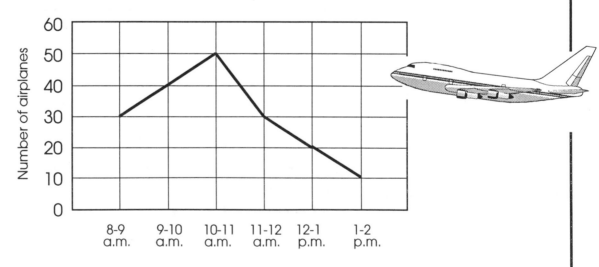

1. During which time period did the most planes land?_____

2. During which time period did the fewest number of planes land?

_____

- What is the average amount of rainfall for your area each month of the year? Use an almanac or other source to find out. Then design and make a line graph that shows the average amount of rainfall for each month. Write 3-5 questions that others could answer by using the line graph.

Ask one of your parents to record the number of miles (s)he travels each day for one week. Use this information to make a line graph.

# Review

Answer the questions about the pictograph.

**Baseball Tickets Sold**

| Frank | 🔴 🔴 🔴 🔴 🔴 |
|-------|-------------------|
| Kim | 🔴 🔴 |
| Miyoko | 🔴 🔴 🔴 🔴 |
| Ricky | 🔴 🔴 🔴 🔴 🔴 🔴 |
| Seth | 🔴 🔴 🔴 🔴 🔴 |

Each 🔴 equals 10 tickets.

1. How many more tickets did Ricky sell than Kim? _____

2. Which two students sold a total of 90 tickets? _____

   _____

Make a bar graph that shows the same information presented on the pictograph.

Answer the questions about the bar graph. Two students, Ann and Reagan, agreed to compare their scores on a series of English tests. The graph shows their scores on six different tests during the grading period.

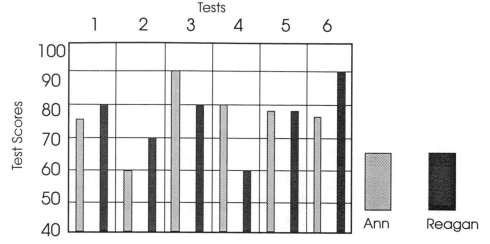

1. On which test was there the greatest difference between their test scores? _____

2. On which test was there the least difference between their test scores? _____

3. On which test was there about 15 points difference in their test scores? _____

Make a line graph that shows the same information presented on the bar graph. The line graph will need two lines.

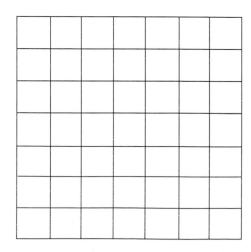

# Achievement Award

This award is presented to

for successfully completing
**Math and More**, Grade 5

Presented this _____ day of _____, 19 ___

by _____
signature